D0390477

BICYCLES

LOVE POEMS

ALSO BY NIKKI GIOVANNI

POETRY

*Black Feeling Black Talk / Black
    Judgement*
Re: Creation
My House
The Women and the Men
Cotton Candy on a Rainy Day
*Those Who Ride the Night
    Winds*
*The Selected Poems of Nikki
    Giovanni*
Love Poems
Blues: For All the Changes
*Quilting the Black-Eyed Pea: Poems
    and Not Quite Poems*
Acolytes
*The Collected Poetry of Nikki
    Giovanni*

PROSE

*Gemini: An Extended
    Autobiographical Statement on
    My First Twenty-five Years of
    Being a Black Poet*
*A Dialogue: James Baldwin and
    Nikki Giovanni*
*A Poetic Equation: Conversations
    Between Nikki Giovanni and
    Margaret Walker*
Sacred Cows... and Other Edibles
Racism 101

EDITED BY NIKKI GIOVANNI

*Night Comes Softly: An Anthology
    of Black Female Voices*
*Appalachian Elders: A Warm
    Hearth Sampler*
*Grand Mothers: Poems, Reminis-
    cences, and Short Stories About
    the Keepers of Our Traditions*
*Grand Fathers: Reminiscences,
    Poems, Recipes, and Photos
    of the Keepers of Our Traditions*
*Shimmy Shimmy Shimmy Like
    My Sister Kate: Looking at the
    Harlem Renaissance through
    Poems*

FOR CHILDREN

Spin a Soft Black Song
Vacation Time: Poems for Children
Knoxville, Tennessee
The Genie in the Jar
The Sun Is So Quiet
*Ego-Tripping and Other Poems for
    Young People*
*The Grasshopper's Song: An Aesop's
    Fable Revisited*
Rosa
*Abraham Lincoln and Frederick
    Douglass: An American Friend-
    ship*
Hip Hop Speaks to Children

BICYCLES

LOVE POEMS

Nikki Giovanni

HARPER  PERENNIAL

NEW YORK • LONDON • TORONTO • SYDNEY • NEW DELHI • AUCKLAND

HARPER ● PERENNIAL

A hardcover edition of this book was published in 2009 by William Morrow, an imprint of HarperCollins Publishers.

BICYCLES. Copyright © 2009 by Nikki Giovanni. All rights reserved. Printed in the United States of America. No part of this book may be used or reproduced in any manner whatsoever without written permission except in the case of brief quotations embodied in critical articles and reviews. For information address HarperCollins Publishers, 195 Broadway, New York, NY 10007.

HarperCollins books may be purchased for educational, business, or sales promotional use. For information please e-mail the Special Markets Department at SPsales@harpercollins.com.

FIRST HARPER PERENNIAL EDITION PUBLISHED 2010.

Designed by Gretchen Achilles

Library of Congress Cataloging-in-Publication Data has been applied for.

ISBN 978-0-06-172649-1

17 18 WBC/RRD 10 9 8 7 6 5 4

Bicycles: because love requires trust and balance

CONTENTS

Blacksburg Under Siege: 21 August 2006   1

In Simpler Times   3

If Only   4

Field Notes   6

Migrations   8

I Am Jazz   11

Shoe Jazz Blue Jazz   12

The 3rd Rail   13

I Am Confused   15

My New Car   16

Dinner At Nine   17

My Muse   19

I Am Glass   21

No Heaven   22

Alchemical   23

Your Shower   25

Good Night   26

My Sleep   28

Bicycles   29

I Like The Dance   31

I Would Not Be Different   32

Give It A Go?   34

Another Day (Revisited)	36
Christmas Laughter	39
I Want A Shoe	41
A Drunken Phone Call	43
A Substitute For You	44
I Know The Song	46
I Am A Mirror	48
Everything Good Is Simple	49
Deal Or No Deal	50
I Provide	52
Gray Clouds Hover	54
I Am The Ocean	55
I Clean	57
So Enchanted With You	59
How To Save The World	61
Free Huey	62
My Beer	64
They Think	66
Why Don't You Love Me	67
First Chair	69
Friends and Lovers	71
Love (And The Meaning Of Love)	72
Flight Delay	73

Travelers   74

Trash Pans   75

Letting The Air Out   76

Fame   79

Duets   81

Boiled Blues   83

Love Luther   86

A Song For You   88

Friends In Love   89

No Translations   90

Twirling   92

Good Books   93

Got A Minute (To Fall In Love?)   95

Where Do You Enter   97

Tourism   99

The Scenic Route   100

Tree Line   101

The Artist   102

A Fish Out of Water   105

We Are Virginia Tech   107

ACKNOWLEDGMENTS

I would like to thank Clinton,
who always seems to make time for me.

BICYCLES

LOVE POEMS

BLACKSBURG UNDER SIEGE: 21 AUGUST 2006
(for Carolyn Rude)

Not safe . . . not even all that nice . . . when you think about it . . .
What mean fraternity boys do with their fists . . . and drunk frater-
nity boys do with their penises . . . barefoot boys do with guns . . .
Whether it's a redneck screaming "nigger" . . . or a poet hollering
"titties" . . . illegal and unkind behavior tells someone s/he doesn't
belong . . . check it . . . check it out . . .

Not nice . . . No . . . And no reason to feel safe

A good day . . . someone pointed out . . . however . . . to be black . . . or
a woman . . . and not be hunted . . . and not have to hold your head
down . . . and not have to quiver . . . when you pass a man . . . po-
lice . . . or professional . . . yet still knowing . . . at any given mo-
ment . . . you are a target . . .

"They didn't move fast enough" . . . they cried . . . "They could have
done more" . . . they demanded . . . "More to let us hold on to our illu-
sions of safe . . . to let us hold on to our illusion of fair . . . to let us hold
on to our illusions . . . illusions . . . illusions" . . . And whether it was a
bullet flying or an animal cracker coming straight at you . . . it was
an attack . . . And yes . . . maybe there could be faster motion . . .
faster lockdown . . . faster dismissal . . . but hey there is the bigger
picture . . . and after all he didn't mean it . . . his leg was sprained . . .
he's so intelligent . . . so talented . . . so special . . . he didn't realize his
heart was blind . . . he didn't understand he was causing pain . . .
Bang! Bang . . . he sang . . . *I shot you Down* but I really didn't have a

gun . . . and just because you're dead . . . doesn't mean I really did it . . .

I shot the deputy . . . hey hey . . . he sings . . . *but I only pretended with the rest of you*

And in the end he was very careful with himself . . . Sure not to be treated the way he treated McFarland and Sutphin . . . Avoiding the knockout blow or killer smile he dealt the man who came when he called *"Help"* . . . Silencing his victims with death for their good-will and sense of decency . . . Or their pity for him . . . Do all the sane and sober things to protect yourself, Monster . . . so that you can plead Innocent By Reason of Not Paying Close Attention . . . Threaten us that you can make Blacksburg not ever be the same again . . .

But we will be the same . . . willful ignorance will overpower indignation every time . . .

That still does not make us nice . . . and it sure doesn't make us safe

IN SIMPLER TIMES

I talk to myself

People think I am on my phone
In simpler days
I would have been considered strange
People would feel sorry
For me
And called me Crazy
I would have walked down the street
Carrying brown paper bags
Arguing   laughing sometimes
Humming a tune

I am alone
At the kitchen sink
Or behind the wheel
Of my car
Taking the roasted chicken
With root vegetables out of the oven
It's easy to see
The delight I am taking
In this life

I am always smiling

I am in love

IF ONLY

If I had never been in your arms
Never danced that dance
Never inhaled your slightly sweaty odor

Maybe I could sleep at night

If I had never held your hand
Never been so close
To the most kissable lips in the universe
Never wanted ever so much
To rest my tongue in your dimple

Maybe I could sleep at night

If I wasn't so curious
About whether or not you snore
And when you sleep do you cuddle your pillow
What you say when you wake up
And if I tickle you
Will you heartedly laugh

If this enchantment
This bewilderment
This longing
Could cease

If this question I ache to ask
    could be answered

If only I could stop dreaming
 of you

Maybe I could sleep
 at night

FIELD NOTES
(On You)

3rd and long
I go for it
4th and short
I jump over the pile

Someone hears a moan
That would be me
Someone heard a sigh
That would be you

A pile of sugar
A pile of salt
I dip my finger
And taste

They said
You hadn't been seen
In over twenty years

They think
You might be
Extinct

I know better

I saw you smile

Rare . . . yes
But still here
Inviting me
To fall
In love

MIGRATIONS

When the sun returns
   to the arctic circle
   from its winter rest

The grasses sprout
   seducing the winged
   and the hoofed

Polar bears and their cubs
   must flee
Before the ice
   breaks up

Although others begin
a northern journey

The Snow Goose flies
   from the Gulf of Mexico
   to mate and birth her young

Two million Mongolian Gazelles move
   over the tundra where each gives birth
   at the same time defying
   the will of predators
   who would consume
   the gazelles' future

Though only, of course,
    to provide nourishment
    for their own
    young predators

Let's not judge
    too harshly

Salmon swim upstream
    jumping falls
    and grizzly bears

Grasshoppers
    ignoring the advice
Of ants
    make music
    to celebrate
Winter's end

Monarch butterflies
    leaving the safety
Of Zihuatanejo
    forge north
Beginning the longest winged journey
    of Spring

With only the hope of warmth
   and the promise of grasses
They unflinchingly face:
     Hunger
     Thirst
     Predators
     Winds
     Rains
     Uncertainties

As would I
For you

I AM JAZZ

I am jazz
I am smooth but not pop
I am cool but not contained
I run the soundtrack
Of your life

You enter me with dissonance
Then command a little rag

There may even be a prayer or two
Somewhere in there

I am jazz

When you are alone
I come to you
Giving you rhythm to work
And rhyme to care

I agree with *pure jazz*
I am safe for your dog
Cool for the cats
Salt in the pond
For your fish

You need me
Admit it
You need me

SHOE JAZZ BLUE JAZZ

Green shoes
Blue shoes
Red shoes
Good news

Bad news
Suede shoes
No ties
Loose pants

Pink shoes
   Shining
White shoes
   Whining
All shoes
   Dining
On the little ants

Your shoes
Her shoes
My shoes
Good news

His shoes
Those shoes
Miles Davis
All Blues

THE 3RD RAIL

I was running
Running running

I wasn't in a hurry
'Cause I didn't have anyplace
To go

I've been in love
Before
And I know
The best thing to do

It's not like I've been
Hurt
And there is way more jazz
Than blues
When I soundtrack
My life

It's just that the time
To persuade
And seduce
Runs into *Law & Order*
Not to mention *Monday Night
Football*
And I do have book club
Garden club

And though I should give up
I am still trying
To train the dog

I also have a job
And dirty clothes
And dinnertime requirements
So I was running
'Cause there just wasn't any
More time in the day
But then you smiled
And I smiled back
And not paying enough attention
I stepped on that 3rd rail

I AM CONFUSED

I am confused

I am in a not so much fog
As gray cloud

I cannot read
The landmarks

Let alone
The *Danger* signs

I do not know

Where I am

Or how I got here

I am lost

I want to find myself

In your arms

MY NEW CAR

I drive
like I have a new car
I don't want anyone
to bump it
or scratch it
or actually get too close
to it
Stay in your own lane
I want to shout
But I stay satisfyingly cool
I fit in
I relax
I don't want you to think
I think
I have any reason
To be jealous

DINNER AT NINE

I am seated
given a wine
and entrée menu

I smile
and happily talk

I nod my head
and let my hands express
      Compliance
      Competence
and a gentle but questioning
      Compassion

People think I am
on the phone
They recognize
I am in love

I order the '04 Malbec
      the baked mussels
      (though my favorite is boiled)
      the sautéed soft-shell crab
      a nice green salad
the bread is hot
and the butter soft

I am comfortable
In this little French restaurant
And made welcome

Yet

When my order arrives
The waiter doesn't understand
Why there is only
me

MY MUSE

I am my own
Muse

I delight me
With my words
Of both wisdom
And wit

I teach myself
So much
Such insight
Into the human
Soul
Such compassion
For the weak and weary
Such utter contempt
For the self-satisfied

I think
What a wonderful world
It would be
If only people
Would listen
To me

I look at the full moon
And bay

Come
Come
Come to me
Let's explore
A new world

I AM GLASS

I am glass
You can see through me
I'm easily hurt
Any little pebble can cause a scratch

I rise in neither love nor need

If you black me out
I become a mirror

If you open me
I am a part of a door

We are all more than our experiences
And less than our dreams

If you blow your breath on me
I can fog

Then you can write your name
Claiming me
For you
For all time
Or
At least
Until the sun shines

NO HEAVEN

How can there be
No Heaven

When rain falls
gently on the grass
When sunshine scampers
across my toes

When corn bakes
into bread
When wheat melts
into cake

When shadows
cool
And owls
call
And little finches
eat upside
down

How can there be
No Heaven

When tears comfort
When dreams caress
When you smile
    at me

ALCHEMICAL*

I am the cricket
In the grass
I talk by rubbing
My wings against
My legs
I am calling   calling   calling
For a friend

I am the spider
Capturing shadows
Weaving this web
To let the light
Dance

I am the harvest moon
That allows you
To read
A midnight
Poem

I am the autumn wind
Whooshing cold
Bringing you greetings
From blankets and fireplaces

*because love is magical

I am that tiny ball of cotton
From your grandmother's quilt
Which tickles
Your nose

I am the pepper
In your soup
The garlic
In your sauce
The taste in your mouth
When you are tired

I am a match

Light me

You need to change

How you look
At things

YOUR SHOWER

I wish I could be
Your shower
I would bubble
Your hair
Tickle my way
Down to your lips
Across your shoulders
And over your back
Around your waist
Bouncing off your knees
Fall to the tips
Of your toes
Then journey back
Again
Warm   Wet
Sticky   Sweet
Up and Down
Around and Around
Around and Around
Around and Around
Until
There is
No more hot
Water

GOOD NIGHT

It is late
I stand
In front of your desk
Saying something inane
You fiddle with papers
Not looking at anything
Work is over yet
We stay

I smile
You are, after all, very cute

We leave the building
Casually
Like it doesn't matter

There is a beautiful moon
We say Good Night

I unhurriedly stroll to my car
Humming some 1950s love song

I speed-limit home
                  to
            Walk my dog
            Give fresh water to the birdbaths
            Eat my dinner

Choose my clothes for tomorrow
Set the coffee timer
Slide between my bamboo sheets
And dream
Of you

MY SLEEP

I appreciate my sleep
In sleep my conversation
is witty
My home is dusted
My office work
is up to date
The dog
is even
well behaved
And food is on the table
on time
But then
when I'm asleep
I don't have you
to clutter and confuse
My hungry heart

BICYCLES

Midnight poems are bicycles
Taking us on safer journeys
Than jets
Quicker journeys
Than walking
But never as beautiful
A journey
As my back
Touching you under the quilt

Midnight poems
Sing a sweet song
Saying everything
Is all right

Everything
Is
Here for us
I reach out
To catch the laughter

The dog thinks
I need a kiss

Bicycles move
With the flow
Of the earth

Like a cloud
So quiet
In the October sky
Like licking ice cream
From a cone
Like knowing you
Will always
Be there

All day long I wait
For the sunset

The first star
The moon rise

I move
To a midnight
Poem
Called
You
Propping
Against
The dangers

I LIKE THE DANCE

I like the dance
I like the idea
    of you in my arms
I like the gentle sway

I like the dance
I like your sweat
    on my cheek
I like the way you breathe

Look at me
Look at me

I like the way I feel
    in your arms

I WOULD NOT BE DIFFERENT

Every now and then
We all fall in love
With a totally inappropriate
Person

And I would not be different

You sort of see someone
And you don't want to notice
That ring on his finger
Nor really that sort of happy
Look in his eyes

You do however know
Immediately
How wonderful it would be
To fall into those arms
To nuzzle the hairs
Of his underarms
To rub your cold feet
Against those thighs

You do want to know
What the water would feel like
As it caresses you two
In a rainbow shower
The soapy suds swirling around
As you kiss and kiss and kiss

You do want to know
How he takes his eggs
Whether his toast should be buttered
On both sides
If he drinks decaf or regular

But he is a totally inappropriate person
And all the world knows
This cannot work

Yet all the world would think
If they could see him
"I want to be in love with that"

And I would not be different

GIVE IT A GO?

I like to polish
Silver
Rub the paste in
Let it set
Then shine shine shine

Even as a little girl
I loved to wash
Grandmother's crystal
Watch the light bounce
Off the edges
Of the glasses

We were taught
Never to use clear
Fingernail polish
But to trim our nails
To a respectable length
And buff them
With lamb's wool

I wipe my bathroom
Mirror after each shower
And always shine my faucet

In order to properly care for things
They must be loved
And touched

Want to give it
A go?

ANOTHER DAY (REVISITED)

Librarians do it
but they do it by the book
Fishermen do it
'cause they have a special hook
Opticians do it
and they love to take a look
Zorro does it
'cause he's a special crook

Three-ring circuses
do it for the clowns
Football players
do it on first downs
Swimmers do it
'cause they know they will not drown
Prince does it
'cause he likes to go down

Chefs do it
and they like to use the spices
Bakers do it
with all the bread that slices
Butchers never do it
on the job
Persnickety folk
never do it with a slob

Weather persons . . . in any clime
Poets do but only in good rhyme

My Mama said No but my Daddy doesn't care
And I really kind of like that thing you play with in
my hair

I do it 'cause you really stole my heart
You do it 'cause that's the natural part

We do it 'cause we're curious
and

We do it
just for fun

But when you did it to me right
my heart became undone

And now you have to do it
'Cause there is no other one
Who can do me who can do me who
can do me
Like you done

Yesterday has left us
Tomorrow may not be
There's no reason to be scared
'cause you're safe with me

'Cause you're safe with me

'Cause you're safe with me

CHRISTMAS LAUGHTER

My family is very small
Eleven of us
Three are over 80
Three are over 60
Three are over 50
Two of us are sons

Come Labor Day the quilts
are taken from the clean white sheets
in which they summered

We seldom have reason
and need no excuse
to polish the good silver
wash the tall stemmed glasses
and invite one another
into our homes

We win at Bid Whist
and lose at Canasta
and eat the lightest miniature Parker House rolls
and the world's best
five-cheese macaroni and cheese

I grill the meat
Mommy boils the beans

Come first snow the apple cider
with nutmeg . . . cloves . . . cinnamon . . .
and just a hint of ginger
brews every game day and night

We have no problem
luring
Santa Claus
down
our chimney

He can't resist
The laughter

I WANT A SHOE

I want a shoe named for me
    The Giovanni
It will make you think of a plot
Type it out faster
And get a cover letter
Quicker
Than you can say "Jack Robinson"

I want a shoe
That will let me float
Down the red carpet
To the cheers of an adoring crowd

High-tops with red strings
Something fashionable
Yet humble

I need a shoe named for me
That keeps my feet at an even 72 degrees
And also oils my heels
And trims my toenails

It shouldn't cost too much
Because I am
After all
Just a poet
Thinking way outside

The box
And . . .
Oh yeah . . .
I need dimples
too

A DRUNKEN PHONE CALL

A drunken phone call
From a middle-aged woman
In the middle of the night
After *SportsCenter*
Reminds me
That life is short
And cold
And mean
And maybe I should
Have called you
Like I said
I would

A SUBSTITUTE FOR YOU

I'm a fan of Christopher Columbus
I want to find a spice route too
They've got a substitute for sugar
I want a substitute for you

I'm gonna ride those trade winds
Find gold in El Dorado too
They've got MasterCards for money
I need a substitute for you

My feet at night
Are so cold
I tell you they're turning blue
They have a substitute for coal oil
I'll buy a substitute for you

Some things are real though most things
Really don't be true
They got a substitute for the truth
But a lie right now won't do

You let me think you loved me
Luckily I can't sue
With work and play we drifted
I'm requesting something new

I'm not saying
This is nice
There's a crack
That love fell through

I'm just saying
What we had is gone

I need a substitute
For you

I KNOW THE SONG

I know the song
The moon sings
Though she only sings
To moonbeams
And to all the stars
That twinkle
In the night

I know the song
Her heart hears
Since she belongs
To no one
And there is none to hear
Her sing her song

I know to sing
The moon song
That mostly the moon
Sings alone
Bravely
Through the night

I know the song
The moon sings
I understand the harmony rings
That tinkle chiming for the sun

I, too, am
A motherless child
My heart and soul
Are running wild

I, too, am a motherless child

I AM A MIRROR

I am a mirror

I reflect the grace
     Of my mother
The tenacity
     Of my grandmother
The patience
     Of my grandfather
The sweat
     Of my great-grandmother
The hope
     Of my great-great-grandfather
The songs
     Of my ancestors
The prayers
     Of those on the auction block
The bravery
     Of those in middle passage

I reflect the strengths
     Of my people
     And for that alone
I am loved

EVERYTHING GOOD IS SIMPLE

Everything good is simple: a soft-boiled egg . . . toast fresh from the oven with a pat of butter swimming in the center . . . steam off a cup of black coffee . . . John Coltrane bringing me "Violets for My Furs"

Most simple things are good: Lines on a yellow legal pad . . . dimples defining a smile . . . a square of gray cashmere that can be a scarf . . . Miles Davis *Kind of Blue*

Some things clear are complicated: believing in a religion . . . trying to be a good person . . . getting rid of folk who depress you . . . Horace Silver *Blowing the Blues Away*

Complicated things can be clear: Dvořák's *New World* Symphony . . . Alvin Ailey's *Revelations* . . . Mae Jemison's ride in space . . . Mingus *Live at Carnegie Hall*

All things good are good: poetry . . . patience . . . a ripe tomato on the vine . . . a bat in flight . . . the new moon . . . me in your arms . . . things like that

DEAL OR NO DEAL
(for ENGL 4714 CRN 16937)

My class is not sure
That I should apply to
Deal or No Deal

They think I am lucky
After all
I am teaching
Them

They know I am smart they are
For example
learning
yet

They don't want to see me
Make those greedy mistakes
And push beyond
The envelope

The banker is neither friend
Nor foe
He's a machine

To think you can beat him
Is to think you will win
At Vegas or love

But I persist

My dream is a red dress
Above my knees
High-heel red sandals
And me coming over the top
The music booming
Hi Howie I will say
With a lovely smile

I don't want to play the game
I want to be it

They were born forty years after me
Yet I am younger

I know you cannot go
Through life
Unless you are willing
For love or money
To make a fool
Of yourself

Where else does the ecstasy
lie

I PROVIDE

I am the stretch
The scratch
The way your shoulders
Shrug off sleep

I am the first note
Of the song you sing
The first beat
Of the rhythm you tap
The only high note
You reach

I am the ink
On your newspaper
The grounds
That make your coffee
The bread
That you will toast

I am your shoelaces
For your run
The towel for your sweat
The seat you recline against
As you catch your breath

I am the salt in your stew
The butter in which you scramble your eggs
The apples that flavor your yogurt

I am the wish
On the flame of your candles
When they sing
"Happy Birthday"
Blow me, baby

I am yours

Everything you need
I provide

Now tell me
Why
You're not happy

GRAY CLOUDS HOVER

Gray clouds hover
The chimes outdoors toll
Water splashes out of the birdbaths
The winter winds swirl fallen leaves

Folklore says if the leaves
Make a circle there will be
A death at that home

I do not worry
I have me to keep
Me warm

February is the shortest
month

I AM THE OCEAN

(for Fifty Women Over Fifty)

I am the ocean . . . it is not the moon that calls me to the shore . . . it is
I who awaken the moon . . . and call him down . . . and rest in his
light . . . that I may dream

I am the sand . . . I hold the ocean in my arms . . . I gently rock this
planet . . . smoothing the rough places . . . leveling the high . . .
raising the lowly . . . always . . . singing a love song

I am glass . . . you can see through me . . . I'm easily hurt . . . any little
pebble can cause a scratch though it takes diamond to cut . . . I can
stand against the storm . . . laugh at lightning . . . let the rain sheet
down . . . Why don't you stay here with me . . . safe and warm

I am more than your past

I am not cotton . . . to be picked and picked and picked until some crazy
boll weevil destroys me . . . I am not peanuts grown underground . . .
harvested raw . . . made into many things . . . nor am I taffy . . . to
be pulled and pulled and pulled . . . made acceptable by artificial
sweetener

I am my own me

If you stand in back . . . stopping the light . . . I become a mirror . . . I
reflect who you wish you were . . . and think you ought to be . . . I
show you who you are not

If you open me I become a window ... I bring a fresh breeze ... to caress you ... to calm the fears

I am a cloud ... I float above all else ... I bring shade from the sun ... I cool your coffee ... I make shapes to form your stories

I am your future

When the waters embrace me ... when the moon glows down ... you clearly see me shining ... I   Am   A   Jewel ... I shine

I am

Priceless ... Incomparable ... Undeniable ... Wonderful

Me

Forever and Always Dreaming

Of you

I CLEAN

I clean ... No ... that's not true. I throw things away. My favorite things to throw away are in my refrigerator. Old, or even just plain ole ugly-looking food, cooked or raw, or anything that no longer appeals to me, Must Go. It's a rule. I just *died* to have that piece of Brie. In the middle of the night I put on my garden shoes and sloughed my way to the store. Found the Brie. Brought it home. 1—forgot to leave it out 2—it didn't ripen 3—now it must be microwaved 4—it will taste as I suppose shit does 5—it must be thrown out.

If there is not enough food, I turn to clothes. The T-shirts that have the least little mark on them. Mother used to say I was just like my father. If I have it on I will polish my shoes, dry the silver, wipe the spot. Then when the T-shirt cannot be cleaned I can throw it away. Sox are a favorite also. There is always something wrong ... a pillie here ... a bit of elastic showing there. Even favorite pink argyles have been sent on to sox heaven. And there are always blouses that you simply must ask yourself: why in the devil did I buy that? The answer is simple: when you get blue you can throw it away. I know, I know, you are asking but what about your cosmetics and pharmaceuticals? I am compulsive so I keep my cosmetics up to date: I have about a three-month supply of hand soap, shower gel, face and body lotion. But my pharmaceuticals? Well, yes, that painkiller *did* expire a bit ago but you can never know when a pain will hit and hey! Vicks smells the same in or out of date. And I've never seen a bottle of peroxide or alcohol that didn't work no matter how long they've been hanging around!

So if those solutions still find me on the down side I pull out my big guns!!! My garden! I attack those weeds with so much vigor that all I can do after an hour or so is come in the house and open that really wonderful bottle of wine I've been saving for when I fall in love again. I'm not in love but drinking a vintage red makes me wish I were. And that definitely lifts my spirits.

SO ENCHANTED WITH YOU

I like
    Boiled turnips
    Boiled potatoes
    Boiled rutabagas
        with butter
        and sea salt
But not every day

I like
    Fried Virginia flounder
    Fried sand dabs
    Fried smelts
But usually only on Friday nights

I want
    Drop biscuits
    Miniature Parker House rolls
    Extra thin white bread
When I uncharacteristically
        make a sandwich

I like
    Garlic straight off the vine
    Anchovies anytime
    And good red wines
        'cause I'm too old
        to drink cheap

I like to pound and grill my veal
I rub my beef
   In a special chili mixture
I really don't eat
     anyone else's ground meat

In other words:
   I'm Normal

So this is the question:
   Why am I so enchanted
    with you

HOW TO SAVE THE WORLD IN 100 WORDS

(for O, The Oprah Magazine)

For me—it is the realization that I cannot save the world.
  The world is neither time nor money.
For me—it is that thing in front of me:
  The man in prison for a horrible crime
  who has become my brother
  My neighbor's sons who talk football to me
  over the back fence
  The yellow jackets who have made their home by my deck
All the things I say I don't have time to do but really
  don't have time to don't do
For me—it is the joy of being alive
For me—it is the living

I clock this in at 99 words. I wonder what I missed.

FREE HUEY

(for *Essence* magazine)

First there was the dream ... though Huey wouldn't call it that ...
Huey would say "A Ten Point Program" ... "Power to the People" ... But the people must dream ... if they are to use Power
effectively ... and to dream you must rest ... and to rest you must
be safe ... So Huey called Bobby called Little Bobby ... Calling
All Men ... All Strong Black Men ... All Men who are weary of
arrest ... weary of disrespect ... weary of dreams deferred ...
Called them all to Sacramento ... in Black leather jackets and
Black tams ... with stern Black faces ... and shiny Black guns.

But the government did not ask Who ... are these Dreamers ... The
government cringed ... before the mirror of its own conceit ... and
goose-stepped up its lies ... Neither lies nor bullets could bring this
Panther down ... Huey said "Let there be Women ... Equal in the
struggle."

And good work was done ... breakfast programs ... schools ... voter
registrations ... hospitals ... a   mayor   elected ... a   governor
confirmed ... the arts and literature extolled ... a newspaper with
all the truth you need to grow not all the news they want you to
know ... And the fear of the government could not be contained.

"Panthers" ... the   government   then   declared ... "are   now
extinct" ... as they photographed Huey on the ground ... a bullet
now firmly lodged in his back ...

"A drug deal"...the government said..."gone bad"...another great government proclamation...right up there with: *the slaves are happy...the single bullet theory...the people will welcome us with open arms.*

This righteous...visionary warrior...who...too...had seen the mountaintop
And heard the hosannas...FREE HUEY...stepped onto a passing cloud...ascending to his rightful place...forever...in our hearts.

MY BEER

I wish I liked beer

I see the ads with the happy
People golden drops swimming
Down to quench
That thirst

They are always so ecstatic

I see the bride and groom
At the reception
Toasting each other
With green glass bottles

The guys at the end
Of golfing:
        Plaid pants
        Spiked spectator shoes
        Clear bottles of dark yellow brew
        With tiny dead worms
        Floating to the top

The women with the tennis
Gear under the table
All having icy glasses
With foaming heads
Laughing laughing laughing

They are always so giggled

I even understand the process:
>Grain hops and all that secret ingredient
>Stuff with glacial water high from snow-
>Capped mountains

Beer I am told is one
Of the foodstuffs of life

It is a metaphor an image
A synonym for contentment

There is, after all, no equivalent
For bourbon   scotch rum or wine
If I could learn to like beer

I could change my life
I'd have somewhere
To put my tears
When we fight

THEY THINK

They think I sleep
Too much
They are worried
I am depressed
Or simply drained
Of energy
And do not know how
To get it back

They cannot see
What I see

That you come
To me
And cuddle near
Telling me stories
And jokes
Kissing my forehead
Making me safe
And laugh

If I don't sleep
I am awake
Alone rambling in a clean
Well-ordered
house

WHY DON'T YOU LOVE ME

Why don't you
Love me

I am good with dogs
And children

Old people like me
'Cause I listen
To their stories

I dress real sharp
My hair looks good
Too
I exercise
Whenever I can

I smile every time
I see you

And say something
Terribly witty
And clever

I just don't understand

I say *Jambo*
When I answer my phone

And *Ciao*
When I hang up

I really really really
Don't know

What more
I can do

FIRST CHAIR

They say I'm too jazzy
For First Chair

I bring something different
And maybe something nice

But the orchestra is Baroque
And I am Gospel

It is Beethoven
And I'm Rhythm and Blues

It's piano
And I'm honking sax

My problem is:
      I make my own muffins
      Ice cream
      And music

Not always the best
But all ways my best

I look good
And I dress well

I definitely have
Stage presence

I want to play
I want to play
I want to play

FRIENDS AND LOVERS

Friends and Lovers
    are different
    things

Friends:
    go shopping for shoes
      with you
    add extra garlic
      to that new tomato sauce recipe
    giggle over that silly thing
      that happened back in high school

Lovers:
    cause your heart to stop
      beating
    put cotton and dumb things to say
      in your mouth
    take you to paradise
and back again
and again
and again

LOVE (AND THE MEANING OF LOVE)

I wanted to
But you couldn't

I hoped
But you wouldn't

I understood
Why we shouldn't

So you declined
And we didn't

But it would
Have been fun

If we would've

FLIGHT DELAY

I uncharacteristically ate
A slice of sausage pizza
And characteristically drank
A regular Pepsi

I characteristically thought
Of you
And uncharacteristically said
To myself

Nobody loves me

I characteristically chastised
Myself
By uncharacteristically sneering

*So what
Everybody can't love you
Anyway*

But I characteristically wanted
You
To uncharacteristically be
Here
In this all too familiar airport
During
A characteristic
Flight Delay

TRAVELERS

I have had good luggage
Beautiful Italian leather
Strong brass handles
Black
And I have seen
How many folk carry
My old brand

I've gone cheaper

A loud yellow
So that it can be easily seen
A semi-hard case keeping
The insides safe
And dry
Sort of like calling you
At the end of the day
Practical but still
A brush-off as you
Need to prepare for your evening
Engagements

I understand

I just wish I didn't
Travel so much
Then I could carry
A good bag

TRASH PANS

A trash pan holds little trash . . .
the grit that falls that's not big enough for garbage . . .
but horrible underfoot nonetheless . . .
not smelly but annoying . . .
needing to be swept away . . .
so that the floor is easier walked upon . . .
with bare feet . . .
so that in the middle of the night the grit . . .
doesn't work its way up my pajama leg . . .
so that I don't turn over . . .
and scratch . . .
and realize . . .
you are not home yet . . .
I need to keep a trash pan near my bed . . .
so that when the lies come . . .
I can sweep them up and take them to the toilet . . .
no sense in letting them stay around . . .
to hurt my feelings . . .
bodies tell untruths with shrugs . . .
smiles . . .
and tongue . . .
maybe there should be a little bitty trash pan . . .
for your little untruthful heart

LETTING THE AIR OUT
(of my tires)

This is not
a country song

I am not
a dixie chick

There is
no creek rising

There is no moon
weeping blood

No hound dog baying

No little old man
at first light
up to catch a speckled trout

I don't have
a pickup truck

I don't do
roadkill

My hair isn't "big"

There's no breast implant

I don't talk
through my nose
or have an American flag
tattoo

This is more pitiful
than Polly
wanting a cracker

Or eggs that won't sunny-side up

Sadder than grits
that won't boil

Or chicken wings
that stick to the skillet

This is me
Letting the air out of my tires

Not loosening the lug nuts

Not taking my spinners off

Certainly not being so rude
as slashing these tires
that have hardly been
properly ridden

Just me gently allowing
the air to escape
but saving that good rubber

Just me bent and crying
admitting the truth

We're not going anywhere

Thank God
for *Monday Night
Football*

FAME

(for my former Football-playing student)

When Fame comes knocking
At your door
You've got to do Fame
And something more

When spotlights up
Your telephone
You've got to answer
Then go alone

It's good to have money
It's good to have friends
But when you add Fame
Then the trouble begins

You've got to have sense
To go with the dollars
Know where to fence
Value the hollers

When you open that package
Of fortune and Fame
Keep your sanity
Keep your good name

You've got talent
And good looks too
And now you'll need
To change your view

Control your family
Control your friends
'Cause this is where
Your new life begins

As Fame comes walking
Through that door
Sure—do the Fame
But have something more

DUETS

I don't do duets

Even as a kid I didn't like
Sharing
I would just as soon
Let you have it
Than cut it in half

I sing solo
Because I'm not good
With harmony

I remember my sister
Wanting to borrow
Some thing
      a sweater
      skirt blouse
      whatever
She could have it

My tennis shoes
Had holes in them
Kept together
By safety pins

I made it cool
To be poor

In another age
I would have been a vegan

I don't play doubles
In tennis
Don't bowl with a league

If I was a fat lady
I alone would sing
At the end

And listen
If you don't
Come home
Soon
I'll be
Very
Disappointed

BOILED BLUES

(for the Mississippi Delta)

I like my blues boiled with a few tears
On the side
I like my men a little crazy
And my women to be good friends
I like my sons bold
And my daughters brave
I am the Mississippi Delta

I like my people black

Nobody understands why they stayed with me
The folks who drained this basin were as mean
As a rattlesnake waking up at dawn

You do not have to take this
Seriously
If you take it seriously
You will sweat the magic
You will blind the magic
The magic will not sing

I want mud on my breasts
And honey on my toes
And something really great
Against my thighs

Come on baby
Come on baby come on baby
Dance with me

Does a nudist wear an apron
When she cooks

I like my water on tap
My beans dried
And hot sauce on my chitterlings

If were a shower
I could saturate your hair
Work my way over your lips
Across your shoulders
Around your waist
Through your knees
To the tips of your toes
And back again
Warm wet salty
Sweet

But I'm a River
Started because an ice field fell in love
With the sun
Started small

You can jump me
In Minnesota
But I ate well and grew

I am the Delta
I am black
And unafraid of the wind
I caress the Crescent City
I bring the blues

This time
I'll take mine fried

LOVE LUTHER

To not love Luther
Is to hate blue skies in summer
Is to disdain the tears of a baby missing her mother
Is to prefer screw top to cork

To not love Luther
Is to want to be bitten
By a rabid fox
Or chased in the night by a hungry mosquito
Or to prefer the silence
Of growing grass
To the mellow voice of love

If the Isley Brothers were the Outlaws
Between the Sheets
Luther was our Mountie riding
The Rolls-Royce of our Dreams

If some insecure Rap moguls
Called us dirty names
Luther elevated us
To Princess of Passion

They say Romeo and Casanova
Were the sultans of love
With a secret technique to drive
Women crazy

Luther knew the main ingredient
Is just to say Stop for Love

A man's smile is aphrodisiac enough

Love, Luther?

We all do

Just as we love Montana skies
With all those shooting stars
Just as we love the smell of rosemary
We have whisked across our pillows
Just as we love the voice that so classically told us
Love
Happens first
Between the ears

A SONG FOR YOU

I sing for you
Out of tune
Off key
Forgetting lyrics
Remembering longing

I perch
On your heart
I whisper in your ear

Tiptoeing lightly
Across your lashes
I steal a kiss

You flick
And blink
And flick
Again

I fly away
Leaving my song
     doo wop doo wop
     doo wop doo ditty ditty wop

FRIENDS IN LOVE

Times change
Jobs change
Friends remain
Forever

We age
We sage
Friends laugh
Together

We sigh
We cry
Friends in love
Completely

Hands and hearts
Tied up as one
In this package
Neatly

NO TRANSLATIONS

the smells of a pot roast from the oven
turnips garlic onions
potatoes celery parsnips
tomatillo yucca root

Jack Frost painting
the windows

my cold feet
your warm back

"It started in New Orleans
  but now it's everywhere . . ." Pure Jazz on your dial

chocolates coffee
a good red wine
18 degrees and falling
high winds
maybe a power loss

giggles laughter
sweatpants jeans

I speak to you
in the language
of love

no translations
necessary

TWIRLING

Grits with Vermont yellow
      cheddar cheese
White toast
      with that single pat of butter
      in the center
A pounded pork chop
      or two
Dandelion greens
      (I wish mustard were in season)
Radishes gently sautéed
      in a mixture of olive oil and chardonnay
      with just a splash of balsamic vinegar
And you
      in the center
Twirling
      'round and around and around

Dance for me, Baby
The pig feet haven't even
      unthawed

GOOD BOOKS

When I grow up I want to be a book. I want to be a blue sky with white fluffy clouds and lots of pretty flowers. I want bluebirds and redbirds and mother robins flying by. Maybe a lazy kitten swatting at butterflies that light on her nose. I will tell the stories of little possums making friends with Mr. Snake. Everybody thought Mr. Snake was mean and grumpy but he had a small cut on his side and he couldn't put a Band-Aid on it. When Zip Mouse and his friends discovered the problem they were brave and helped Mr. Snake. Grandmother will put me on her lap and read my stories until the children fall asleep dreaming peppermint dreams. They will learn to be brave.

As I grow older I will be a bigger book. I will gather all the words and definitions for words and definitions of the defining and people will come to me when they need to know something. I will have pictures and examples and maps and formulas. I will show them seven continents; I will present riddles (*Cup and saucer. Saucer and cup. Where does a hole go when it's filled up?*) I explain there are seven seas and two big oceans. There were glaciers and dinosaurs. Alexander the Great thought he had conquered the world. He didn't even get halfway there. Earth thinks it is the only life in the universe, we haven't been far away enough to know. I will ask questions: Why do we have wars? Why are people hungry? There will be times people will not like me. I will be banned and forbidden. But I will be brave. I will stand for light and truth.

And when I am old I will be the oldest book. I will sit on Grand-father's lap and tell The Greatest Story Ever Told. The children will be dressed for bed and I will sing a psalm or recite a proverb. I will try to always be a good book. And the children will dream good dreams of good people trying to do good things.

GOT A MINUTE (TO FALL IN LOVE?)

what I'm trying to
make clear is:
I've saved you so
much stress and strain
I saved time
and money too

I talked
to your secretary
and checked
with your schedule

I brought coffee
to your assistant
and sent flowers
to your mom

I keep jerky
    for your dog
lint remover
    for your suits
And even a neutral
color shine
    for your shoes

I always have
    a nail file
and musk lotion
    for your hands

And did you notice
the brown leather chair
for you to relax
in when you stop
by my office

Stick 'ems
and stop 'ems
Clarify
Consistent

I am perfect
for the job

I save you time
and money:

Got a minute
to fall
        in
            love?

WHERE DO YOU ENTER

Where do you enter
A poem

At the same place
I enter you
with balance
and trust
and a jazzy sense
of adventure

Painting outside
the lines
wearing clothes cut
against the bias
with spices
among the flowers

A poem unfolds
like a baby bat
testing her wings
or a kitten taking
her first steps
or a good dog
moving arthritic limbs
toward the door

There is sadness
as well as loss
in the promise
of love

We begin a poem
with longing
and end with
responsibility

And laugh
all through the storms
that are bound
to come

We have umbrellas
We have boots
We have each
    other

If I may quote Labelle:
Voulez-vous coucher
Avec moi? Ce soir?

TOURISM

I am always a tourist

No matter where
I am

At home
Or abroad

An American
   in Aruba
A Black
   in Oxford
A woman
   in Baghdad
Alone
   cruising
The Panama Canal

Cold in Alaska
Comfortable only
   when the plane
Lands

Never sorry
Yet never safe

In your arms
or out

THE SCENIC ROUTE

MapQuest is
No help there
Are too many
Bumpy back roads
That they call
The Scenic Route
And not enough four-lanes
To quickly come
To conclusion

I follow the curve
Of your smile

You turn flicking
Your signal
And I
    paying scant attention
Go straightaway
Past the *Detour* sign

Though I am
Drowning
You never
Look back

Didn't you notice
I was following
you

TREE LINE

We live above the tree line

If we stand
Tippy toe we can
Reach into the Milky Way
And run our fingers
Around the rim
Of that chocolate pot
Others call the Black Hole

This night is made
For walking
Holding your hand
Having a crescent moon
Laugh down on us

There are things
Flying around
Even at this height
Where it should be
So cold only ice
And snow grow

Yet there is something
Evergreen
About this love
That I
Offer you

THE ARTIST

And so it comes
To this

The sun beating
Down

The people indifferently passing

And we . . . out
Of breath
In a pool of salty
Sweat
Laughing   Happy
In each other's
Trust

That once again
We gentled the stone
All the way down
And will now

Push it back up

But we will wait
Until the sun sets

We will wait
Until the stores
Close

We will wait
While they put their garbage bags
In the streets

We will wait
Until the dogs and rats
Sniff their choices

We will wait
Until the street cleaners
Push their brooms
And the women offer their wares

We will hope
The men are kind

We will salute
The moon rising

We are Sisyphus

We write the poems
We paint the portraits

We sculpt the statues
We quilt the blankets
We set the tables
We make the beds
We wipe the tears
We rock the anger
We hold on to tomorrow

We push the rock up
And we gently bring it down

We were promised
Only a gift of light

You keep me
From being
Lonely

A FISH OUT OF WATER

I know how
The mermaid
Feels

You give up
Your gills
So you can't
Go back
To the water

Yet there is
No way
You can live
On land

There are cats
And dogs
And even robins
Who might take
Pleasure
In capturing
Something strange

There are school
Children
Who will
Throw rocks

And laughter
At the little
Fish who
Floundered

There is of course
The memory
Of the love
That propelled
This jet

And now I sit
On the beach
Listening to the waves
Crash over the rocks

And wish
I had seen
The end of this story
At the beginning
Instead of
At the end

WE ARE VIRGINIA TECH
(16 April 2007)

We are Virginia Tech

We are sad today
We will be sad for quite a while
We are not moving on
We are embracing our mourning

We are Virginia Tech

We are strong enough to stand tearlessly
We are brave enough to bend to cry
And sad enough to know we must laugh again

We are Virginia Tech

We do not understand this tragedy
We know we did nothing to deserve it

But neither does the child in Africa
Dying of AIDS

Neither do the Invisible Children
Walking the night away
To avoid being kidnapped by a rogue army

Neither does the baby elephant watching his community
Be devastated for ivory
Neither does the Mexican child looking
For fresh water

Neither does the Iraqi teenager dodging bombs
Neither does the Appalachian infant killed
        By a boulder
        Dislodged
        Because the land was destabilized

No one deserves a tragedy

We are Virginia Tech
The Hokie Nation embraces
Our own
And reaches out
With open heart and mind
To those who offer their hearts and hands

We are strong
And brave
And innocent
And unafraid

We are better than we think
And not yet what we want to be

We are alive to imagination
And open to possibility
We will continue
To invent the future

Through our blood and tears
Through all this sadness

We are the Hokies

We will prevail
We will prevail
We will prevail

We are

Virginia Tech

ALSO BY NIKKI GIOVANNI

ACOLYTES
ISBN 978-0-06-123131-5 (hardcover)

Giovanni aims her intimate and sparing words at family and friends, as well as at the deaths of heroes and friends, favorite meals, candy, nature, libraries, theatre, and more.

BLUES: FOR ALL THE CHANGES
ISBN 978-0-688-15698-5 (hardcover)

From the environment to our reliance on manners, from sex and politics to love among black folk, these fifty-two poems, published in 1999, offer something for every soul and every mood.

THE COLLECTED POETRY OF NIKKI GIOVANNI: *1968–1998*
ISBN 978-0-06-072429-0 (paperback)

The complete volumes of: *Black Feeling, Black Talk/Black Judgement, My House, The Women and the Men, Cotton Candy on a Rainy Day,* and *Those Who Ride the Night Winds.*

LOVE POEMS
ISBN 978-0-688-14989-5 (hardcover)

Romantic, bold, and erotic, Giovanni's 1997 *Love Poems* expresses notions of love and intimacy in ways that are delightfully unexpected, and includes more than twenty new poems.

THE NIKKI GIOVANNI POETRY COLLECTION
ISBN 978-0-06-051429-7 (audio unabridged CD)

THE PROSAIC SOUL OF NIKKI GIOVANNI
ISBN 978-0-06-054134-7 (paperback)

Giovanni's adult prose, including: *Racism 101, Sacred Cows . . . and Other Edibles,* and *Gemini: An Extended Autobiographical Statement on My First Twenty-five Years of Being a Black Poet.*

QUILTING THE BLACK-EYED PEA: *Poems and Not Quite Poems*
ISBN 978-0-06-009952-7 (hardcover)

Giovanni's 2002 revelatory gaze at the world in which we live—and her hopeful poems depicting a world she dreams we *will* call home.

Visit www.AuthorTracker.com
for exclusive information on your favorite HarperCollins authors.

Available wherever books are sold, or call 1-800-331-3761 to order.